MW00879221

The 97% Swing Trade

*Learn a Swing Trading Strategy
for Beginners With a
97.71% Win Rate*

1St Edition

By Tim Morris

ISBN: 9798861616225
Published by ZML Corp LLC

Table of Contents

Disclaimer

This book is written for informational and entertainment purposes only. The creator of this book is not an investment advisory service, a registered investment advisor, or a broker-dealer and does not advise clients on which securities they should buy or sell for themselves. It must be understood that a very high degree of risk is involved in trading stocks. The publisher and author of this book assume no responsibility or liability for trading and investment results. It should not be assumed that the methods, techniques, or indicators presented in this book will be profitable nor that they will not result in losses. In addition, the indicators, strategies, rules and all other features of the information presented are provided for information and educational purposes only and should not be construed as investment advice. The title and subtitle of this book are in no way a guarantee of trading results, and success rates can differ for all traders, meaning there is the potential to make nothing, or even lose money performing this strategy. Please do not place any of this strategy in the review section of Amazon, or your account will be reported and your review will be deleted. Copyright © 2021, all rights reserved. Written by Tim Morris. Published by ZML Corp LLC.

Introduction

Hi and thanks for being here. My name is Tim Morris and in this book, I will show you a simple swing trading strategy which I have coined, *The 97% Swing Trade*. I named it this because, as you may have guessed, this trade comes with a 97.71% win-rate. You may be skeptical of my claims, as there are a lot of "promises" on the internet (Extenze still hasn't kept their promises to me).

What I ask of you is to read the entire book, understand the concepts behind the strategy, the reasons why it works, and then try it out on your own. If you follow the rules that are laid out in this book, I think you'll be pleasantly surprised with the results and the consistent profits this strategy provides. Now I'm not going to make any crazy claims like you'll become a millionaire overnight or get a date with Kate Upton (she still hasn't messaged me back on Facebook). However, I do feel you'll be very happy with the results and discover a simple swing trading strategy you can start using yourself... a swing trade that actually works!

One other thing I'll mention is I don't fluff up my books to make them 300 pages long. You'll notice most of my books are 100 pages or less. I understand people have busy lives and you don't have time to drudge through chapters about my prior life as a Shingon Monk or what Warren Buffett eats for breakfast in the morning to find out what the book is about. So while my books are shorter compared to other authors, I stick to the point; hope that is appreciated.

Chapter 1

Terminology

This strategy involves certain stock terminology, charts, and indicators that some traders may be unfamiliar with. For this reason, let's first go over the information which will help us better understand the concepts behind this strategy.

Candlestick Charts

Many traders may be familiar with classic "line charts," as shown below in a chart of Walmart (WMT).

However, line charts only show the *closing* price of a stock on any given day. What line charts fail to show is the opening price, high price, and low price a stock made on that same day. And this is where **candlestick charts** become a helpful tool.

Candlestick charts relay much more information to traders versus ordinary line charts, which can help with different trading strategies (such as the one in this book). If we look at the image below, we can see the different aspects that go along with a "candlestick."

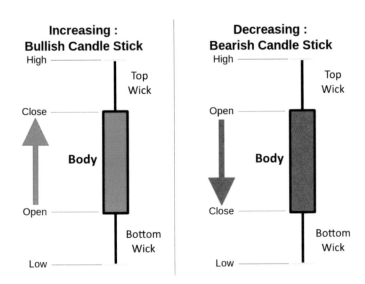

As you can see, the **body** of the candlestick displays the opening and closing price of a stock during a given time interval, while the **wicks** display the high and low it made during that same time interval. And depending on what color the body is determines if the stock moved higher in price (*green candlestick*) or lower in price (*red candlestick*) during the time interval displayed.

That's something else to note about candlesticks, in that you can use them in different *time intervals*. Most stock software defaults to a "daily" time interval when displaying charts. However, the time interval can be changed to 5 minutes, 1 hour, 1 week, etc.

For example, say you pulled up a candlestick chart and set the time interval to 5 minutes. Now, instead of showing candlesticks that correspond to one day's worth of price action, the candlesticks will now correlate to 5 minutes' worth of price action. As in, each candlestick is showing the open, close, high, and low corresponding to each 5 minute period of a given trading day.

While the strategy outlined in this book will just be using *daily* time interval candlesticks, it is still beneficial to know that time intervals can be changed. This is so you can choose the correct time interval when viewing a chart.

Below I have an example of the same Walmart line chart shown previously, except this time in candlestick format. A daily time interval was chosen, meaning each candlestick represents one day's worth of price action.

Shorting

While you will be buying stocks the majority of the time using the strategy outlined in this book, there may be times you instead want to short a stock.

Shorting is essentially "selling" a stock first, and then buying it back at a later time. This allows you to make money as a stock moves *down* in price. You're able to short a stock because brokers allow clients to "borrow" shares from other traders in order to sell them. This may be a little confusing, so let me provide an example that makes the idea of shorting easier to understand.

Gold is currently priced at $1,000 an ounce, but you think gold will go down to $500 an ounce in the near future. You have a friend who has an ounce of gold. You ask your friend if you can borrow his gold, and you will pay him 5% interest for the time you borrow it. Your friend lends you his ounce of gold, and you immediately go to the open market and sell it for $1,000. Six months later, gold is priced at $500. You go back to the open market and buy an ounce of gold. You then give this ounce of gold back to your friend, along with the interest fees you promised him. You end up profiting $500 on this trade, minus the interest fees.

This example is essentially what happens when you short a stock, except "your friend" is another trader, and the "open market" is the stock market. The fees I brought up are "shorting fees" which vary depending on the stock you choose.

Stocks that have a lot of short interest, as in many traders shorting the stock at the same time, can sometimes go through a situation known as a "short squeeze." This tends to occur when a stock starts rising in price rapidly, and traders who are shorting the stock close their positions to avoid losing additional funds. Because you have to *buy* a stock to close your position after you have shorted it, the flood of short sellers closing their positions actually pushes the stock price higher, thus creating a domino effect where more shorts in turn buy the stock to close their positions as well.

Indexes

Indexes are "baskets" of different stocks that track a particular sector of the market. As in, they are used as a "proxy" to show how different sectors of the market are performing. There are thousands of different indexes in the United States, with some well-known indexes being the NASDAQ (technology companies), the S&P 500 (500 largest companies), and ARCA Gold (gold mining companies).

When an investor looks at one of these indexes, she can see how a particular sector of the market is doing. In this book, we will be focusing on another common index known as the Dow Jones Industrial Average, commonly called the "DOW" or "DOW 30."

This index tracks 30 "blue chip" companies trading on the New York and NASDAQ stock exchanges. A blue chip company is slang in the stock market world for a reputable, large-cap, stable company with many years of success. Think Microsoft or McDonalds. These are companies that have been around a long time, with little chance of going out of business, even during hard times in the market.

And it is for this reason that stocks in the DOW are the main stocks traded using the strategy in this book. Swing trading is of course more risky than long-term investing, however trading blue-chip companies such as those in the DOW greatly increases the odds that our swing trades will be profitable.

Order Types

There are different types of orders you can place when you go to buy a stock. While we will be primarily using *stop-limit* and *stop-loss* orders, all of the orders mentioned in this section are still important to understand.

Market Order

As you may be aware, stock prices are actually the middle of the "bid/ask spread." Buyers put up a bid, sellers put up an ask, and the middle of this "spread" is shown as the stock price.

So if stock XYZ has a bid of $10.19, and an ask of $10.21, it's price would be shown as $10.20. If you were to put in a *market order* to **buy** stock XYZ, it would execute at the first available ask price from a seller, which in this case would be $10.21.

Stocks with large amounts of trading volume, such as those in the DOW, typically have small bid/ask spreads. Meaning that using market orders is typically not an issue. Market orders tend to be a poor choice when trading stocks with *large* bid/ask spreads.

Limit Order

With a *limit order* you are telling the broker the maximum you are willing to pay for a stock, and not a cent more. So again, if stock XYZ is trading for $10.20, and you set a limit order for $10.05, only when the stock moves lower and a seller offers an ask of $10.05 will the stock be purchased.

If you were to set a limit order at a price higher than $10.20, say $10.30, your order would execute immediately. This is because you just told your broker the max you are willing to pay for the stock is $10.30, however the next available ask price is $10.21, which of course is below $10.30.

Stop-Order

A *stop-order* may be a new concept to some traders. This is because, unlike a limit-order, you are telling your broker the *least* you are willing to pay for a stock. As in, you are telling your broker you won't buy a stock until it reaches a *higher price* than it is currently trading for. So once again, stock XYZ is trading for $10.20. You could set a stop-order at a price of $10.50. Then, only when XYZ rises to $10.50 will your order get executed. And it is actually executed via a market order. As in, once the price of stock XYZ reaches $10.50, your broker executes a market order, buying the stock from the next available seller.

The downside to strictly using a stop-order is you don't have exact control of what price you will buy the stock. If there is a large bid-ask spread on the stock, your broker could potentially purchase the stock for $10.52, $10.55, etc., depending on where the "ask" resides once the stock reaches a price of $10.50.

Stop-Limit Order
A *stop-limit order* is the **main order type** we will be using in this book. As the name implies, it is actually two orders in one, meaning you are setting two prices with this order. The first is the "stop" price, which is a *higher* point than where the stock currently resides. The second is the "limit" price, which is the max you are willing to pay for the stock *after* it has reached your stop price.

So again, let's say we want to purchase stock XYZ at a price of $10.50, but it's currently trading for $10.20. We would put in our stop-limit order, with a stop price of $10.49, and a limit price of $10.50. Then, once the stock reaches a price $10.49, our broker would now put our limit order into the market at a price of $10.50, which would likely be executed in a short time-frame. As in, once the price of the stock reached $10.49, the most we would pay for the stock would be $10.50.

The stop-limit order gives us more control over the price we pay for a stock, versus using just a stop-order by itself.

If the stop-limit order is perplexing to you, it will make more sense once we go over examples later in the book.

Stop-Loss Order
When swing trading, there are times when you want to cut your losses and close out a losing trade; this is where a *stop-loss order* comes into play. It essentially tells your broker you want to sell your position when a stock *declines* to a certain price point.

For example, say we bought stock XYZ at $10.50. The stock starts moving downward, and we're concerned losses may persist into the future. We can put in a stop-loss order at $10.10. Then, if the stock were to continue declining and touch $10.10 sometime in the future, our broker will automatically sell the stock for us, thus preventing any further loss.

Gap Downs
There are certain times when a stock opens lower than the price it closed at the day before; this is known as a *gap down*. A gap down occurs when the stock price changes during the after-market hours (*4pm-8pm*) and/or the pre-market hours (*4am-9:30am*). These gap downs can occur for a variety of reasons including a poor earnings

announcement, changes in company management, a government policy which affects the sector, etc. The candlestick chart below shows an example of a gap down which occurred on a stock chart of Caterpillar (CAT).

The image above is a *daily* candlestick chart, as in each candlestick represents one day's worth of price action. As you can see, CAT closed at $239.41 on May 18th, and opened at $236.10 the next day on May 19th. This $3.31 difference is the amount the stock *gapped down* between its close on May 18th, and its open on May 19th.

Chapter 2
Strategy Outline

As many traders know, stocks go through their ups and downs. They rise one minute, and fall the next. However, if you were to place a moving average line on the chart of a large cap company, such as one in the Dow Jones Industrial Average (DOW), it tends to revert back to its mean. Knowing this, we can use it to our advantage.

The basis behind the strategy I present in this book was originally developed by *Larry Williams*, a famous stock and commodities trader. He came up with the idea in 1979, and coined it the "Oops Strategy." Larry states he named it this because when a broker would report to his clients that they were stopped out, the broker would call and say, "*Oops, we lost.*"

The philosophy behind this trade is after stocks gap down, especially stocks that are held in high regard (*e.g. blue chips*), they tend to revert back to their mean. And when a stock starts moving up quickly, such as after a gap down, traders who were bearish tend to cover their shorts and get out of their position. The occurrence of this "short squeeze," as well as buyers who want to get into the stock at a lower price, are the key reasons why this strategy works. We are then using the ensuing momentum to *swing trade* the stock and make a profit

With Larry William's strategy being the main concept behind this book, I have refined it in a way that makes it a higher probability trade. This is because I have added three tactics to the strategy to improve upon it which include:

1) *Only trading stocks in the DOW*
2) *Waiting until the first profitable opening to exit*
3) *Using a wide stop-loss*

Adding in these three concepts, I was able to improve both the net gains, as well as the win-rate, statistics we'll go over more in chapter six. In the image below, I have a list of the 30 companies that currently represent the DOW Index:

Company	Symbol	Year Added	Company	Symbol	Year Added
3M	MMM	1976	McDonald's	MCD	1985
American Express	AXP	1982	Merck & Co.	MRK	1979
Amgen	AMGN	2020	Microsoft	MSFT	1999
Apple Inc.	AAPL	2015	Nike	NKE	2013
Boeing	BA	1987	Procter & Gamble	PG	1932
Caterpillar Inc.	CAT	1991	Salesforce	CRM	2020
Chevron Corporation	CVX	2008	The Coca-Cola Company	KO	1987
Cisco Systems	CSCO	2009	The Home Depot	HD	1999
Dow Inc.	DOW	2019	The Travelers Companies	TRV	2009
Goldman Sachs	GS	2013	The Walt Disney Company	DIS	1991
Honeywell	HON	2020	UnitedHealth Group	UNH	2012
IBM	IBM	1979	Verizon	VZ	2004
Intel	INTC	1999	Visa Inc.	V	2013
Johnson & Johnson	JNJ	1997	Walgreens Boots Alliance	WBA	2018
JPMorgan Chase	JPM	1991	Walmart	WMT	1997

Finding Stocks to Trade

To begin, we have to first find stocks in the DOW that have gapped down **and** are below their previous day's low. This is an important concept; the gap down needs to be *below* the previous day's low.

To find these "gappers," you can use a free website called FinViz (linkpony.com/finviz). Detailed examples showing how to use this website will be discussed in the next chapter.

There is no "minimum amount" the stock needs to gap down for this strategy to work; it just needs to gap down *and be* below the low of the previous day when it opens. And when I say low, I am referring to the actual low from the previous day, *not* the "close."

Remember with candlestick charts, the close on a downtrending stock is the bottom of the candle *body*. The low that stock made on the day, and **what we are referencing** for this strategy, is the bottom of the candle *wick*. I have an example below detailing this in a chart of Bank of America (BAC).

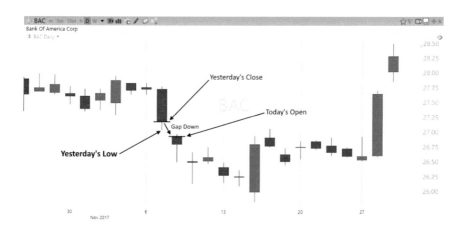

Notice in the image above that Bank of America gaps down and opens *below* yesterday's low. Yesterday's low is the bottom of the candlestick **wick**.

Once you find a stock that has gapped down *below* the previous day's low, you will place a *stop-limit order* at the previous day's low. As mentioned in chapter one, a *stop-limit order* just basically means your broker will not purchase the stock until it moves back *up* and actually touches the price that you specify. This is important as you don't want to buy said stock until it gets to that specific point, being the previous day's low. And once it does reach that point, it is likely to continue moving higher due to the momentum which precipitates it.

There are two prices you put in with a stop-limit order, the first being the *stop price* and the second being the *limit price*. If you're trading any reputable company, the bid/ask spread will likely be within a penny or two, so you don't have to worry too much about a large spread. I usually place the limit price 3 cents above the stop price.

In the Bank of America example from before, the previous day's low point, November 7th, was $27.02. Being that the stock opened on November 8th at $26.92, it experienced a gap down. Seeing the gap down, we would have placed in our stop-limit order at $27.02/$27.05. After this, we then needed to wait for our order to get executed. Sometimes it takes a few hours, sometimes a few days, and sometimes even a few weeks before it comes back to touch this point. In the BAC example, a little over a week went by before the stock moved back up in price and our order was executed (as shown in the photo below).

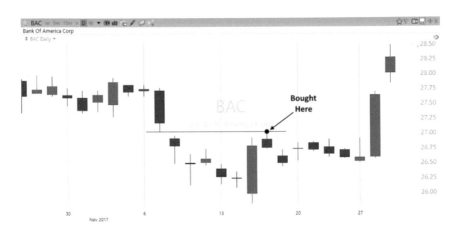

Stop-Loss
Once your limit-order is executed, you have the option to put in a

stop-loss to prevent losses. Based on testing, a stop-loss of 20% appears to be ideal. Closer than this (*e.g. 5%*) and you will get stopped out more often, resulting in less winning trades. Farther than this (*e.g. 30%*) barely moves the needle on the win-rate, and it could then take weeks or even months before the stock comes back to your entry-point. This results in capital being tied up which you could be using on other trades.

The 20% stop-loss is also beneficial from a psychological stand point. It provides a concrete rule to go along with this strategy, as opposed to guessing and worrying where you should exit a losing trade.

In the Bank of America example from before, our trade was triggered at a price of $27.02, meaning our stop-loss order would have been placed at $21.62, twenty percent below our entry-point. Prior to selling the stock for a profit, it reached a low of $26.40. As in it didn't come anywhere near our stop-loss, a typical scenario for this trade.

Taking Profits

In regards to taking profits, you want to exit on the **first profitable opening** (**FPO**). My testing has shown taking profits on the FPO provides the highest returns for this strategy.

This means, even if the stock moves past your entry-point during normal trading hours, you should wait to sell until it has actually *opened* higher than your entry-point. Sometimes this can happen the next day, but other times the stock can move past your entry-point during normal trading hours, but not actually have a profitable opening until a few days after that. I have the BAC example shown again on the following page, except this time with two profit taking scenarios.

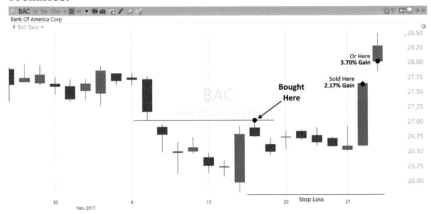

Selling the same day the stock pushed past our entry-point, we would have profited *2.17%*. However, waiting to sell until the **FPO**, as outlined in the rules, resulted in a profit of *3.70%*.

Chapter 3
Trade Examples

Just to reiterate, when you first begin using this strategy, you should stick to trading stocks within the Dow Jones Index for reasons already mentioned. A gap down, especially during normal market conditions, is consistently "filled" by stocks in this index. As you become more comfortable with the strategy, you can branch out to stocks in other indexes if you choose. In this chapter we will be going over examples with stocks that are in the DOW. In the next chapter, we will go over examples with stocks in other indexes.

As mentioned in chapter two, we can find stocks which have gapped down using the *FinViz Screener*. To find stocks using FinViz, you would perform the following steps:

1) *Go to the FinViz screener page (*<u>*linkpony.com/finviz*</u>*).*

2) *Choose "DJIA" from the dropdown menu next to the word "Index" in the middle of the page.*

3) *Click the "Technical" tab at the top of the page.*

4) *Choose "Down" from the dropdown menu next to the word "Gap" on the right side of the page.*

You will now have a list of all the stocks that have gapped down on the current day you are searching. You are looking for stocks that are **still trading below** the low point they made one day before the gap down occurred. For example, if stock XYZ gapped down on August 2nd, you'd be looking at the August 1st low point to see if:

1) *The stock gapped down below this level and if*
2) *The stock is still trading below this level*

Depending on what time you are searching, before the market opens or after market hours, will determine what gappers are still below their low points.

Though tempting, you **<u>do not</u>** want to put in a buy order for stocks that have already passed this low point, as you are then chasing.

Chasing is a cardinal sin in swing trading, and your results will differ from what is outlined in this book.

Depending on your experience level, your account size, and how much you trade will determine the amount you want to risk on each trade. When first starting, I highly suggest using a very small amount of money, or even just a practice account (which I have links to in chapter 6). You never want to risk your entire account on a single trade, as even with the high win-rate associated with this strategy, there are still a few losers. And considering this is more of speculative type of trade, as in not long term investing, I would stick to the rules I bring up in my free report *Crush the Market*. And that would be using a max of 10% of your funds on speculative, swing trades.

Let's go over a few examples of this strategy in action using stocks in the DOW. The companies we will be trading include Apple (AAPL), American Express (AXP), and Nike (NKE).

Example #1: Apple (AAPL)

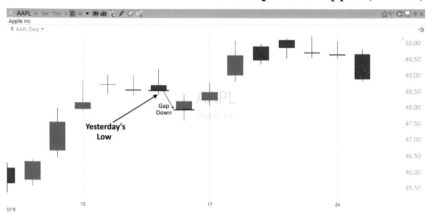

In this example, Apple closed at $48.54 on Thursday, June 13th. The next day (Friday) it gapped down, opening at a price of $47.94.

When viewing the chart, we can see Apple opened on Friday, June 14th *below* June 13th's low point of $48.40. Considering this, we put in a stop-limit order at $48.40 and waited for it to trigger. The following Monday, June 17th, Apple rose in price, executing our order. We would have immediately put in a *stop-loss* at $38.72, twenty percent below our buy-in point.

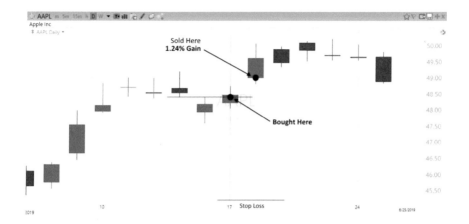

On Tuesday, June 18th, the day after our order was executed, Apple had its FPO when it opened at a price of $49.00. At this point we sold our position, resulting in a **1.24% gain**.

Example #2: American Express (AXP)

In this example, American Express (AXP) closed at $60.06 on Friday, June 24th. On Monday, June 27th, when the market opened, American Express had gapped down to $59.10. We put a stop-limit order into place at $60.00, which was Friday's low. Three days later, on Thursday, June 30th, our stop-limit order was executed. At this point we put in a *stop-loss* for $48.00, twenty percent below our entry-point.

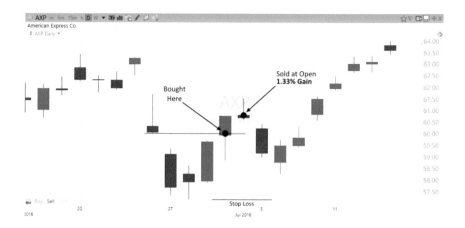

On Friday, July 1st, the day after our stop-limit order was executed, AXP opened at $60.80 (its FPO). We immediately sold, resulting in a **1.33% gain**. Notice we didn't sell the same day it pushed higher than our order, but instead waited until the **FPO**.

Example #3: Nike (NKE)

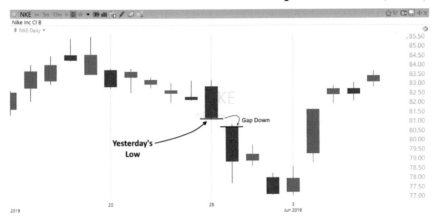

Here, Nike closed at $81.20 on Tuesday, May 28th. When the market opened on Wednesday, May 29th, Nike had gapped down to $80.71. We put in a stop-limit order which correlated with Tuesday's low, at a price of $81.13. On June 4th, six days later, our order was executed. We then placed a *stop-loss* at $64.90, twenty percent lower than our buy-in price.

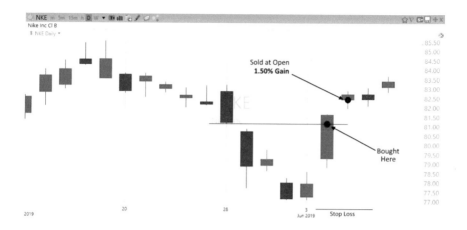

On Wednesday June 5th, the day after our order was executed, NKE had its FPO, when it opened at a price of $82.42. At this point we sold our position, resulting in a **1.50% gain**. Notice again, we did not sell on the day it broke through our buy-in price, but waited until the FPO.

Free Gift

As a **token of appreciation** to my readers, I am offering my special report titled *Crush the Market* **absolutely free**. In this report, you will be provided with 14 incredibly beneficial tips I have learned throughout my trading career which will help you profit in the stock market. Just go to the link shown below, put in your email address, and it will be immediately sent to you!

linkpony.com/crush

Chapter 4
Outside the DOW, Shorting, and Risks

Trading Stocks Outside the DOW

When using this strategy as outlined, as in only trading stocks inside the DOW, the average *win-rate* is very high, while the *net gain* on each trade tends to be rather conservative. Though sometimes higher, you can expect to earn around 1% on each trade.

However, when trading more volatile stocks, such as many outside of the DOW Index, net gains can be much higher. Volatility of course means more risk, but with more risk comes more reward. Let's go over a couple examples.

Example #1: Advanced Micro Devices (AMD)

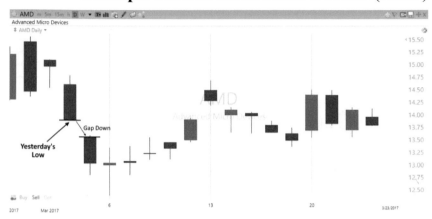

In this example it is Thursday, March 2nd. AMD made a low on the day of $13.87, before closing at $13.90. The next day (Friday), AMD gapped down, opening at a price of $13.55. Noticing the gap down, we put in a stop-limit order for $13.87 (Thursday's low).

It took one week but on Friday, March 10th, our order was executed. At this point we would have put in a *stop-loss* for $11.10, twenty percent below our buy-in point.

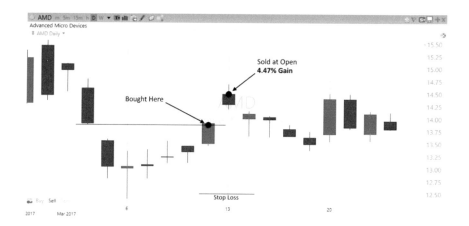

The Monday that followed our buy order, March 13th, AMD opened at $14.49 (its FPO). At this point the stock was sold, resulting in a gain of **4.47%**.

Example #2: Snapchat (SNAP)

In this example it is Monday, May 3rd. Snapchat made a low on the day of $58.64 before closing at $59.17. The following day (Tuesday), Snapchat gapped down and opened at a price of $58.03. A stop-limit order was put into place for $58.64 (Monday's low), and we patiently waited. Three weeks later on Monday, March 24th, our order was triggered. A *stop-loss* order was placed at $46.91, twenty percent lower than our entry-point.

On Tuesday, March 25th, the day after our order executed, SNAP opened at $60.47 (its FPO). We would have sold our position resulting in a **3.12% gain**.

As you can see, the gains can be higher when trading stocks outside of the DOW, however this is because they are more volatile, which means more risk. Something else to note is, while in these examples the stocks had their FPO the day after our orders were executed, it sometimes takes a few days before the FPO occurs.

Trading stocks outside the DOW may be something to consider trying first in a practice account. The broker *Webull* offers a free practice account to traders, and even has a weekly "paper trading" competition where they give away gift cards to the winners. Use my link and receive two free stocks just for opening an account with *Webull* (linkpony.com/webull).

Risks

The main risk associated with this strategy is of course if a stock which you have purchased does not increase in price, but instead loses value and takes out your stop-loss. Considering the rules I present though, as in only trading companies in the DOW Index, as well as only trading in neutral and bull markets, this is a *very* rare occurrence, which the statistics in chapter 6 prove.

I have an example of a failed buy-in below with the company Home Depot (HD).

Here, Home Depot closed at $228.51 on Friday, March 6th. The following Monday, March 9th, the stock gapped down, opening at $213.50. Seeing the gap down, a stop-limit order was set at $222.25, the March 6th low. On Tuesday, March 10th, our stop-limit order was executed. A *stop-loss* was then put into place for $177.80, twenty percent below our buy-in price.

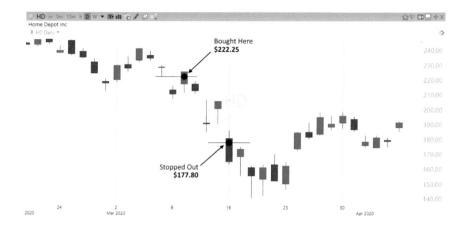

Six days after our order executed, on Monday, March 16th, Home Depot gapped down *again*, opening at a price of $180.92. It then proceeded to move lower through the day, taking out our stop-loss in the process.

In this example, after our stop-loss was executed, Home Depot continued moving downward for another week, and didn't come back to our original entry-point until over one month later.

While 20% is quite a bit to lose on a trade, a loss like this could have been *avoided*, so as long as you watched the news once a week and didn't live in an underground bunker. This trade happened right in the middle of a huge stock market crash, an occurrence that, along with corrections, would be an inappropriate time to use this strategy.

So in summary, the biggest risk with this trade is getting taken out by your stop-loss. However, as long you stick to the rules laid out in this book and follow the overall market health, it should be a rare scenario.

In chapter six, we will go over more ways to limit being taken out by our stop-loss.

Short Selling

As mentioned in the beginning of this book, you can perform "short selling" with this strategy, as opposed to going long. This would mean just flipping around the strategy, and shorting stocks that have *gapped up*. You would then use the *high* the stock made the day before the gap-up as your entry-point.

For the most part, I would not suggest using the strategy presented in this book to short sell *except* for in certain scenarios. For example, let's say a failing company such as SEARS announces they are getting a new CEO and the stock gaps up 10% overnight. This news is most likely hot air, and a failing company like this will likely come back down in price. In this scenario, short selling SEARS would make sense to do.

The second scenario where shorting may be appropriate would be during a poorly performing market (*e.g. a correction or crash*). In this case though, I would abstain from short selling quality companies, such as those in the DOW. Instead, look for weaker companies which are more likely to decline after a gap up, and stick to a 20% stop-loss.

If you are enjoying this book, could you please leave a review? It would be greatly appreciated. Here is a shortened link to the Amazon review page:

linkpony.com/swing

Chapter 5
Summary of Strategy

Step 1: Scan for Stocks

You're looking for stocks in the Dow Jones Index which have:

    i)   Gapped down below their previous day's low *and*

    ii)   Are still trading *below* this low point

For those with full time jobs, scanning at night will allow you to view stocks that have gapped down but have not yet risen above this low point. For those with more time on their hands, scanning right before the market opens will provide you with a wider range of choices, as many times gap downs can occur in the pre-market hours. Once you find a stock to buy, put in a **stop-limit order** at the pre-gap-down low and then wait for your trade to execute.

Step 2: Execution

Once your trade is executed, immediately put in a *stop-loss* order 20% below your entry-point, and then start monitoring your trade more closely.

Step 3: Take Profits

You will take profits on the *first profitable opening*. This means the stock has to not just surpass your purchase price, but actually *open* higher than it. To check for the FPO, pull up your brokerage account a few minutes before the market opens each day and look at the pre-market price.

You could also set an alert to trigger when the stock has crossed above your purchase price. This way, if the stock opens above your purchase price, your alert will go off. The broker *Webull* mentioned previously has an alert feature built into it.

If it is getting close to 9:30am and the stock is trading above your purchase price in the pre-market hours, put in a *market order* to sell. Then, when the stock market opens at 9:30am, your stock will be immediately sold, thus selling at its first profitable opening.

During this whole process, you should be **monitoring your trades**. Some trades may take many days, or even weeks to trigger, or to reach their FPO. You should monitor all your outstanding trades regularly to know how your stocks are performing. Setting alerts is a helpful strategy when your orders are out in limbo for some time.

Chapter 6
Complete Statistics

The win-rate for this trade, which I will go over later in this chapter, is quite high. And based on what you've read so far, I think you can see why. We're taking large cap, blue-chip companies, and going long *only when* they have risen back up to their low point following a gap down. We're not trying to "time" the bottom or going for enormous gains. Instead we're taking conservative, 1%-2% profits with each trade. These two factors, as well as the upward momentum when we purchase the stock, are what gives this strategy so much success.

What's nice about a high win-rate like the one associated with this strategy is it's easy on most traders, especially from a psychological standpoint; it feels good to consistently profit on your trades.

During neutral and bull markets, it's best to use this strategy with stocks that have gapped down, as they are likely to move higher. Corrections and bear markets become a time to either abstain from using this strategy, or possibly short-sell stocks that have gapped up. I discuss how to tell when a bear market is coming in my book *The Crash Signal* (linkpony.com/crash).

Trends and Commodities

Some companies in the Dow Jones Index correlate with commodities or other services, with one example being Chevron correlating with the price of oil. Depending on how not just the market is doing, but also the *commodity*, can determine how a stock price will move. For example, if the market was doing well but the price of oil was getting hammered, Chevron would be a poor stock to trade at that time.

Also you want the stock you are trading to be in a long term uptrend. So before entering a position, be sure to pull up a long term chart of whatever stock you are planning to trade. If the stock has been *downtrending* for many months, and then gaps down, it will likely continue downtrending into the future, even if it happens to rise back up to its previous low point. This of course means it's more likely to take out your stop-loss, making it a poor trade to partake in.

Scanning for Trades

Some days when you scan for trades, there will only be a few stocks that appear. Other days, there will be a ton. You then have to use your own judgement to pick one which you feel will give you the highest probability of being a winner. Again, here you would want to do a little research by checking how the overall market is doing, looking at the long term trend of the stock, and also checking the performance of whatever commodity/service the stock correlates with (*e.g. Chevron with oil*).

An item that hasn't been touched on, and something you want to avoid when using this strategy, is a stock that has made a *parabolic move*. This is where, for one reason or another, a stock has extraordinary gains in a small period of time. These "parabolic moves" end up reverting back down quickly, as a stock cannot shoot into outer space forever. I have an example of a parabolic move on the next page, with the company IBM, which is a part of the Dow Jones Index. Here, IBM moved up over 16% within 5 trading days. On the 6th day, a gap down occurred, resulting in a potential entry for this strategy.

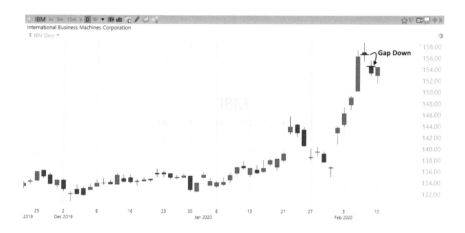

But would this be a good trade to enter? Is IBM going to continue moving higher? Maybe... but probably not. In this scenario, IBM actually ended up dropping from a high of $158 down to $90 within a few weeks. Avoid trading parabolic moves like these.

Paper Trading

When first using this strategy, especially if you are new to trading, I would start by "paper trading." This is where you use virtual money to test the strategy and gain experience before using your real funds. A lot of people lose money in the stock market; you don't have to be one of them! Paper trading will allow you to learn the strategy, fine-tune it to your liking, and then employ it with your actual broker once it has become profitable for you. As mentioned previously, the broker *Webull* (linkpony.com/webull) includes a practice account you can use to test this strategy before deploying your real money.

Strategy Statistics

Compiling data from the last 10 years, from July 2011 to July 2021, here is how this strategy fared only buying stocks in the DOW based on what stop-loss was used:

The 97% Swing Trade Statistics

Stop Loss	Win Rate %	Avg Days Invested	Annual % Gains	Average Profit %
20%	97.71%	10 Days	17.50%	0.53%
10%	93.56%	n/a	9.62%	n/a
5%	86.29%	n/a	5.54%	n/a

As you can see, the 20% stop-loss had a 97.71% win rate, while the win-rate declined the smaller of a stop-loss used. So while you could use a 10% or 5% stop-loss in an effort to save money, and while still profitable, you end up losing out as the win rate and annual gains decline greatly.

Also, the *average profit %* listed is slightly misleading, as it's actually higher. The 20% stop-losses pull down the profit average in the statistics. So in reality, the real average profit percentage you can expect to make on winning trades comes out to **1.02%**.

Here are the individual winners and losers:

Individual Winners

	Stock	Statistic
Highest Total Profit	NKE	373.38%
Highest Win Rate	MSFT	100%
Highest Avg. Profit	NKE	1.10%

Individual Losers

	Stock	Statistic
Lowest Total Profit	CVX	-34.01%
Lowest Win Rate	CVX	94.54%
Lowest Avg. Profit	CVX	-0.08%

Full statistics can be found at linkpony.com/98211. If a password is required, type in "74215".

Something else to mention is these numbers were compiled with *all* stocks in the DOW, including downtrending stocks, as well as when the market was going through corrections and crashes. Had you abstained from using this strategy during corrections and crashes, the annual percentage gain jumps up to over 28%. Fundamentally, this means the strategy could be improved *even more*.

Factors such as not trading stocks below their 20 day moving average, not trading stocks during corrections or crashes, only trading the top 10 stocks in the DOW, using options, etc. could potentially make a great strategy *even better*. These are all factors which will be considered should a 2nd edition of this book be made in the future.

I hope you enjoyed this book and the new swing trading strategy I have provided to you. Used effectively and with the right stocks, this strategy can be a great money making addition to your trading repertoire.

Feel free to reach out to me with any questions you have at tim@trademorestocks.com. I respond to all emails and my grandma says I'm a nice guy. Also, I post informative stock videos on my YouTube channel quite frequently, a link to which can be found on my website at *TradeMoreStocks.com*. I wish you the best in your financial endeavors!

If you liked this book, you may also enjoy…

The 20% Solution
A Long Term Investment Strategy Which Averages 20.13% Per Year

Shortened Link to Book:
linkpony.com/20

You read that right, **20.13% per year**! This strategy, which I have coined *The 20% Solution*, requires just 4 trades a year. This book includes over 30 years of history of this strategy in action, with charts and figures to back it up! Go to the link above to find out more.

The Crash Signal
The One Signal that Predicts a Stock Market Crash

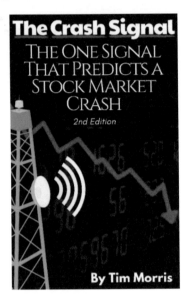

Shortened Link to Book:
linkpony.com/crash

Stock market crashes are inevitable, but losing money **doesn't have to be**! In this ground breaking book, Tim Morris exposes the one signal that has flashed before every stock market crash for the last 60 years. He goes into detail explaining how to prepare for the crash, & even how to make money while it's happening! Save yourself from the next crash with *The Crash Signal*!

ONE-ON-ONE STOCK COACHING

Get the Help You Need to Make Long Term Profits in the Market!

Shortened Link to Webpage:
linkpony.com/coach

Need a little help with your portfolio? **Tim has you covered!** By signing up for a coaching session, Tim will sit down with you for a one hour phone call, where he lays out a customized plan for you to start generating income in the markets. Tim explains how the markets operates, the best portfolio allocation, and the reasons why the long term strategy he will go over with you works so well. When you're finished with your coaching session, you'll have a better understanding of the stock market and a defined plan for your financial future. Find out more at the link above now!

The Green Line

Buy the Bottom of Any Stock Market Correction (2nd Edition)

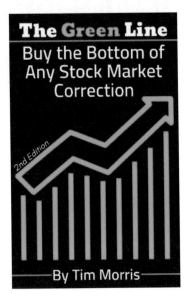

Shortened Link to Book:
linkpony.com/green

A correction in the stock market occurs on average once a year. *What if* you could capitalize on this drop by getting in near the very bottom and selling near the very top? In this book, Tim Morris shows you how to do **just that**, letting you in on a little known indicator which he has coined *The Green Line*. Find out more by going to the link above.

Made in the USA
Columbia, SC
31 October 2024

45374925R00031